DISCARD

Published by Creative Education
123 South Broad Street, Mankato, Minnesota 56001
Creative Education is an imprint of The Creative Company

Designed by Stephanie Blumenthal
Production Design by Sharan Stevenson/Envision

Photographs by Derek Fell

Library of Congress Cataloging-in-Publication Data

Fell, Derek
Herbs / by Derek Fell
p. cm. — (Let's Investigate)
Includes glossary and index
Summary: Briefly describes different herbs, their
cultivation, and various uses.
ISBN 1-58341-002-3
1. Herbs—Juvenile literature. 2. Herbs—Utilization—Juvenile literature. [1. Herbs.] I. Title. II. Series.
III. Series: Let's Investigate (Mankato, Minn.)
SB351.H5F43   1999
581.6'3—dc21   98-11608

First edition

2 4 6 8 9 7 5 3 1

HERBS

DEREK FELL

Creative Education

HERB
ORIGIN

Most herbs, lavender for one, originate from lands around the Mediterranean.

H erbs are a group of plants with useful purposes—usually as flavorings in cooking, but also for healing. Additionally, there is a large group of herbs grown for perfumes and for dyes. The term "spice" is the dried product of an herb plant, such as the hot spice called chili powder, which is derived from the dried fruit of an herb known as the chili pepper plant. During the Renaissance period in Europe, herbs and spices were valued so highly that merchants opened up special "spice routes" by land and sea from their places of origin. It was the prospect of finding a shorter spice route from Europe to India that caused Columbus to set sail across the Atlantic Ocean toward America.

Above, spices at a market in Morocco
Right, safflower
Opposite, wild lavender

HERB
BEAUTY

Many herbs have extremely beautiful flowers; for example, nasturtiums and scented leaf geraniums are often used in flower gardens.

Above, nasturtiums
Right, dill

KINDS OF HERBS

The most common herbs used around the home are **culinary** herbs such as parsley, sage, thyme, dill, basil, chives, and mint. All of these are used as flavor enhancers.

Parsley has fine curly leaves that grow into a cushion shape. It is usually chopped very fine and sprinkled over soups and salads or cooked fish. Cooks also use parsley as a decorative **garnish** wherever a colorful green touch is needed.

Sage has gray felt-like leaves and is valued as a flavor enhancer for many soups, especially those containing meat.

In English-speaking countries, coriander is also known as Chinese parsley and cilantro; it is used to add flavor to soups and salads.

*Left, common basil
Below, coriander*

Thyme grows into a low, mounded shape with tiny pink flowers, and it is most often used to improve the flavor of vegetable soups.

Dill grows tall, with feathery blue-green leaves and an umbrella-shaped flower cluster. The finely chopped leaves are often used to improve the flavor of fish, while the seeds are used in pickles and to flavor cooked cabbage.

Basil comes in many forms, including a variety with purple leaves. Since it grows quickly from seed, basil is a good choice for growing in a pot. Basil is best used with tomato dishes such as pizza, and to make pesto—a **piquant** paste that can be spread on bread.

HERB
FOR CATS

Cats like the herb known as catnip; a cat will happily play for hours with toys filled with catnip.

Right, chives
Below, comfrey

Chives are a variety of onion, growing slender leaves and clover-like pink flowers. The leaves are chopped fine to add an onion flavor to potatoes and especially to cream cheese.

9

Mint has an uplifting fragrance that will clear blocked sinus passages, but the leaves can be steeped in boiling water to make a refreshing tea. Mint sauce is also valued for improving the flavor of lamb.

*Left, spearmint leaves
Above, blossoms on a
spearmint plant*

HERB
USE

Dating back to at least 4000 B.C., herbal **incense** is one of the earliest herb products.

*Above, St. John's wort
Right, an herb garden
and fountain*

HERBAL MEDICINE

The healing power of herbs has been recognized by humans since the dawn of civilization. The first cultivated crops may have been the opium poppy—the source of a dangerous drug that induces sleep. In Medieval times, **monasteries** were places of learning and healing as well as religious devotion, and no monastery was without its **physick** garden—a walled-in area to grow plants that were used to make medicines.

Though much of the claims for herbal remedies is now considered folklore with little scientific evidence, many herbs do have proven medicinal properties. Some of the medicinal uses involving herbs are so **potent** that it is considered unsafe to try them except in the care of a physician. Digitalis, for example, is a medicine that is derived from foxgloves. It is used as a heart stimulant, but improper doses can be fatal. Other herbs can be ingested to relieve certain discomforts. For example, ginger tea will help to settle an upset stomach and ward off colds, and bergamot is an ingredient of Earl Grey tea, a popular beverage taken as a mild energy stimulant.

HERB
HISTORY

The earliest known list of useful herbs was compiled by the Chinese Emperor Shen-Nong, written about 2800 b.c. A similar Egyptian list dates to 1550 b.c.

HERB
FACT

Many herbs developed their distinctive flavors and aromas as a deterrent against being eaten by insects.

Sweet false chamomile is used to make tea

HERB

The discovery of America yielded many new vegetables (such as potatoes, tomatoes, pumpkins, and corn) but few new herbs and spices were found.

Right, aloe vera
Below, common chicory

The **gel** of an aloe plant (taken from inside the leaves) has long been used to treat burns, including sunburn. Smoothed gently on irritated skin, it has a soothing, healing effect. Garlic is known to relieve a toothache when a **clove** is pressed onto the offending tooth, while ginseng—a wild plant growing in the North American woodland—has been proven to restore energy.

HERB

FLAVOR

Many herbs have edible flowers, including nasturtium which adds a pleasant peppery flavor to salads.

HERB

MINTS

In addition to spearmint and peppermint, there are some mints that smell and taste like lemon and pineapple.

Garden nasturtium

HERB

CURE

Aromatherapy is the use of fragrant plant parts to improve health. This includes breathing, bathing, and massaging with fragrant oils.

14

Cauvin Farm in France

HERB FARMS

In addition to farms growing a wide variety of herbs for supplying home gardens, herb farms are devoted to producing one particular herb. In the south of France, for example, the town of Valensol is the center for lavender oil production, an important ingredient in the manufacture of fragrant soaps and perfumes. Ideal for growing lavendar, the gritty soil around Valensol has excellent drainage. The mild winters and dry summers are also good for lavender, the world's most widely grown herb plant.

HERB
VALUE

It takes 72,000 crocus flowers, picked by hand, to produce one pound of saffron spice, making it the world's costliest herbal product.

HERB
USES

With more than 200 species, members of the onion family have the largest number of herbal uses.

Saffron crocus

The costliest herb in the world is the saffron crocus, the source of a spice called saffron. Produced mostly on herb farms in Spain and Kashmir (India), saffron grows in well-drained sandy soil and enjoys mild winters. In autumn when the crocus flowers bloom, they produce scarlet filaments from the center of each flower, which must be removed by tweezers. In dried form, this spice imparts a pleasant bitter flavor to many **gourmet** foods such as the Spanish rice and chicken dish called *paella*, and the famous French seafood soup called *bouillabaise*.

The town of Gilroy, in northern California, is famous for its production of garlic. Each year at harvesting time, the town celebrates with a Garlic Festival. Garlic likes plenty of moisture to fatten up its edible bulbs, and coastal mists around Gilroy help to provide the right amount of moisture.

HERB
USE

The juice from garlic and chili peppers is such a potent insect repellent it can be sprayed on garden plants to protect them from pests.

Left, garlic
Above, hyssopus

HERB
FLOWERS

There are many varieties of thyme, an herb used to flavor meat dishes. Most produce masses of small flowers on low, spreading plants suitable for growing in rock gardens.

**Right, mother-of-thyme
Above, salvia**

One might think that dandelions would grow well anywhere in the world, but the state of New Jersey is the dandelion-growing capital of America, and it celebrates the harvesting of dandelions by holding a festival and electing a "Dandelion Queen." The greens are used for salads, and the flowers are brewed to make an **invigorating** herbal tonic.

A lot of plants are not needed to provide the flavors and spices for an average household. The oils in herbs are highly concentrated, so a little can go a long way. A fragment of a clove of garlic, for example, is enough to flavor a dish of cooked vegetables, while a single bay leaf is all that is needed to add its spicy flavor to a gallon of soup.

HERB
SEED

A good way to grow a large collection of herbs inexpensively is to start them from seed. Seed trays filled with a peat-based potting soil are ideal for getting the seeds sprouted.

19

*Left, young plants started in small seed trays called flats
Below, laurel*

HERB

Parsley is extremely hardy and can survive freezing weather; however, it is not long-lived, and once it goes through a winter it develops seed and dies.

Right, plain leaf parsley
Below, common basil
Opposite, Chinese chives

Many useful herbs—like parsley, basil, and chives—are small enough to be grown in flower pots on a sunny windowsill. Tender herbs—like ginger and aloe—can grow indoors, protected from winter freezing.

HERB
CROWDS

Many herbs tolerate crowding, meaning the plants like to grow tightly together; they are best harvested when young.

**Above, cardoon
Center, herb garden
featuring phlox, viola,
and dianthus**

Outdoors, the easiest way to have an herb garden is to create a raised area of soil in a sunny spot. Plant an assortment of varieties "shoulder-to-shoulder" (most herbs will tolerate crowding). A useful collection of six or seven plants can occupy just a few square feet of space. Parsley, summer savory, and chervil are all easily grown from seeds sown directly into the garden for harvesting within a matter of weeks.

At the other extreme, it's possible to create complex "knot gardens" where a wide assortment of hardy perennial herbs is grown as low hedges to form ribbons and patterns, with annual herbs planted in the spaces between. Fast-growing herbs such as basil and chervil are annuals and need planting from seed each year, but hardy perennials such as mint and chives will come back year after year.

HERB
GARDEN

The idea for knot gardens—using hardy perennial herbs to create low hedges—is believed to have started in Elizabethan England.

Knot garden

23

HERB
CARE

Since many herbs look alike (it is very difficult to tell chervil and coriander apart, for example), it's important to use labels for identification in a garden.

Below, lemon balm
Right, herb garden

Because many herbs are plain-looking, without exotic flowers, most herb gardens rely on the design to make them look attractive. A popular herb garden design is to grow the herbs in geometric shaped beds (square, rectangles, and triangles, for example) with brick paths separating the beds.

When using herbs fresh, select the leaf tips for the best flavor since older leaves and stems can become fibrous. Snipping the plants repeatedly from the top of the plant will do no harm, since this simply encourages side shoots. One of the best uses for fresh herbs such as parsley, chives, oregano, and basil is to chop them fine and sprinkle them into scrambled eggs or to make an herbal omelette.

HERB
FACT

Though most herbs grow best in full sun and in soil with good drainage, watercress will grow with its roots permanently immersed in shallow water.

25

*Left, varieties of basil
Above, jars of dry herbs*

HERB
USES

Lemon grass is used to flavor Oriental dishes with a lemon flavor. When rubbed on the skin, it repels pesky insects.

Right, lemon and herb iced tea
Above, herbal vinegars

Herbs can be steeped, or soaked, in white **vinegar** to make flavorful herbal vinegars. They can also be chopped and pressed into butter to make piquant herbal butters. Brewed in boiling water like tea leaves, they make delicious herbal teas. Hot mint tea is a particularly pleasant beverage if you are suffering from a cold because the steam from the brew will help relieve **congestion.**

26

A "Dyer's Garden" is an herb garden that grows plants which yield colorful dyes for decorating fabrics. Goldenrod, for example, is the source of a yellow dye.

Left, dried herbs and arrangements
Above, blue false indigo

lthough most herbs are good to use fresh, their flavors are often intensified upon drying, allowing them to be stored for long periods. The usual method for drying herbs is to hang them upside-down in bunches and allow them to air dry. After a week they will be dry enough to cut or crumble into smaller pieces and to store in air-tight jars. To speed the drying process, herbs can be spread on a cookie sheet and placed in an oven.

French tarragon can be grown only from cuttings. Russian tarragon can be grown from seeds, but it has an inferior flavor.

Opposite, Greek oregano
Left, herb garden "guarded" by a peacock
Below, teasel

Variety selection is important when choosing herbs. Some varieties of thyme, for example, are odorless and flavorless, but English thyme has a spicy flavor. Similarly with oregano, some varieties have only mild flavors, while the variety known as Greek Oregano has the zesty flavor many people like to sprinkle on pizza.

Florence fennel

A culinary herb is classified as a vegetable when it is considered a food staple and not merely used in small amounts as a flavoring. Leaf fennel, for example, is considered an herb, while the bulbous fennel (a variety that produces an edible swollen stem, often served as a side dish at meals) is classified as a vegetable. Culinary herbs are now so popular they can be purchased fresh at the supermarket produce counter, while dried herb products are widely available from cosmetic stores and bed and bath shops.

In addition to making food taste better, many herbs produce pleasant fragrances. A single sprig of lavender can be placed under a pillow to create the illusion of waking up in a field of lavender. Several sprigs placed in bath water will make it smell pleasant.

Orris comes from the root of an iris. In powdered form it is used as a "fixative," preventing herbal fragrances from quickly losing scent.

When a lot of fragrant herbs are mixed together to create an uplifting aroma, it is called a potpourri. Most potpourris include dried lavender flowers and rose petals. Mixed and placed in a decorative bowl, they can fill a room with fragrance. Herbs have a long history, and as we continue to find new uses for them, they will undoubtedly keep adding flavor, fragrance, and health benefits to our lives.

Left, rose geranium
Above, orris roots

Glossary

A **clove** is a wedge-shaped piece taken from a garlic bulb.

Congestion is an abnormal accumulation or obstruction, usually of the nasal passages.

The word **culinary** refers to something that is used in cooking.

Fermentation is a chemical change in the liquid and causes a **pungent**, or strong, aroma and flavor.

A **garnish** is an herb used to decorate foods.

A **gel** (short for gelatinous) is a jelly-like substance found inside the stems and leaves of many desert plants.

Gourmet food is carefully prepared with well-chosen herbs or spices, and is usually especially good.

Incense is a product made from herbs that releases a pleasant aroma when burned.

An **invigorating** food or beverage boosts the body's energy or overcomes fatigue.

Monks live and practice their religion in **monasteries**.

An herb garden with plants grown especially for healing can be called a **physick**.

Food that is **piquant** has a sharp, appetizing flavor.

If an herb has a strong, powerful dosage, it is a **potent** herb.

Vinegar is a sour liquid produced by fermentation that improves the flavor of many bland, or plain, foods, especially pasta and seafood.

Index